Guru Nanak: First of the Sikhs
© Demi 2021

Wisdom Tales in an imprint of World Wisdom, Inc.

Library of Congress Cataloging-in-Publication Data

Names: Demi, author.
Title: Guru Nanak : first of the Sikhs / Demi.
Description: Bloomington : Wisdom Tales, 2021. | Audience: Ages 4-8 |
Audience: Grades 2-3 | Summary: "Guru Nanak (1469-1539) is the founder
of the Sikh religion, which has over 25 million followers worldwide. As
a young man, he embarked on an inspired mission that took him from the
sacred Himalayas to the holy city of Mecca, preaching a message of one
God, sincere worship, and of peace and equality for all. Award-winning
author, Demi, recounts the remarkable life of Guru Nanak, who today is
revered by Hindus and Muslims alike"-- Provided by publisher.
Identifiers: LCCN 2020037036 (print) | LCCN 2020037037 (ebook) | ISBN
9781937786892 (hardback) | ISBN 9781937786908 (epub)
Subjects: LCSH: Na nak, Guru, 1469-1538--Juvenile literature. | Sikh
gurus--Biography--Juvenile literature. | Sikhism--History--Juvenile
literature.
Classification: LCC BL2017.85.N36 D46 2021 (print) | LCC BL2017.85.N36
(ebook) | DDC 294.6092 [B]--dc23
LC record available at https://lccn.loc.gov/2020037036
LC ebook record available at https://lccn.loc.gov/2020037037

Printed in China on acid-free paper.

For information address Wisdom Tales,
P.O. Box 2682, Bloomington, Indiana, 47402-2682
www.wisdomtalespress.com

GURU NANAK
First of the Sikhs

DEMI
✦ Wisdom Tales ✦

Guru Nanak was born on April 15, 1469 in Talwandi, India, to a Hindu family. A brilliant light surrounded the little boy, who was joyous and laughing gaily, not crying like other babies. The Hindu fortuneteller said, "This child is the incarnation of God, descended to redeem the world. The great prophet has come! All will revere Nanak! The name Nanak will be known throughout the earth and the heavens!" Nanak would become known as the founder of the Sikh religion, which believes in the worship of one God, treating everyone equally, honest work, sharing, and service.

In India the times were very dark. Muslims and Hindus were fighting, and men and God were divided.

A rigid caste system separated the Hindus, promoting blind faith, superstition, and empty rituals. And the Muslims imposed harsh shariah laws in the most rigid ways.

Guru Nanak would become a great spiritual reformer who proclaimed the unity of one God and all men.

Kings have become butchers.
In the darkness of the evil night
Goodness has fled and the
    moon of truth
Is nowhere to be found.

At five years of age, when his Hindu teacher said, "There are many gods and goddesses who provide for us," Nanak replied, "There is only one God, Lord of the universe. He is the sole creator and provider."

When his Hindu teacher said, "There are four main castes, *brahmin* (priest) is the highest and *shudra* (laborer) is the lowest," Nanak said, "All humans are equal. Only our own actions can uplift or lower us!"

When his Hindu teacher said rituals will wash away your sins and appease the gods, Nanak responded, "Rituals are unnecessary. Repeat God's true Name to cleanse your soul. Fill your heart and soul with love for Him."

Nanak loved the beauty of nature and all of God's creation.
With his best friends, Mardana, who could play the *rabac*,
and Bala, who could play the *tabla* drums, they spent all
their days singing songs in praise of God.

But Nanak's father
thought that Nanak
was daydreaming
too much
and needed
to know
business,
and so
he gave him a
job watching
over his cattle.

Once, Nanak fell asleep while the cattle strayed into a neighbor's field and ate up all the wheat. The neighbor complained bitterly to the authorities, but when his field was inspected, they found that not even one blade of wheat had been eaten. Truly a miracle had happened in restoring all the neighbor's wheat!

Still Nanak's father wanted Nanak to learn business. He gave Nanak twenty silver coins to trade in the market place and make a good profit. But when Nanak came across a group of holy men called *sadhus*, who were so thin their ribs were sticking out, he immediately spent all the coins buying food for them.

When Nanak's father heard of this trade he was furious. But Nanak said, "You asked me to make a profit, and so I traded the money for the blessings of the holy men. What better, or holier, trade could there be?"

Nanak was sent back to work in the fields where he sang praises to God all day.

> Make your body the field,
> your mind the harvester.
> Sow the seeds of goodness.
> Let modesty be the water.
> Irrigate it with God's Name.

And every evening many villagers joined in singing Nanak's hymns to God almighty. This was the beginning of Nanak's congregation.

On August 24, 1487, when Nanak was just eighteen, he married a beautiful girl named Sulakkhani from a nearby town. The ceremony was simple and joyous. In time two sons were born: Sri Chand and Lakhmi Das. The family seemed to live on God almighty's blessings alone, as Nanak had saved no money, but had given it all to charity.

Every morning Nanak would bathe in the Bein River before singing God's praises. One day he did not return and everyone thought that he had drowned. But Nanak had been called to heaven by *Akal Purakh*, the almighty God beyond time and death. There in absolute beauty, Nanak saw all creation singing God's glories. The almighty God spoke to Nanak:

"Return to the universe, sing my praises and repeat my true Name, IK ONKAR, and say: 'There is but one God, the sole supreme Being, and the ultimate reality. True is His Name.' Nanak! My true form and my divine light are in you! Travel far and wide and inspire people to repeat and contemplate my true Name!"

In 1496, when Guru Nanak was twenty-seven, he felt the time had come to spread his message of one God, universality, and equality to many lands. He said, "I am not abandoning my family and renouncing the world. I am traveling on an inspired mission. One day, I will return to my family again."

So began twenty-five years of traveling throughout India, Sri Lanka, Nepal, Bhutan, Arabia, Persia, and Afghanistan.

One day
Nanak was
asked to join
two Muslims
praying in
the mosque.
As both men
knelt, Nanak
stood watching
them, reading
their thoughts.
The men asked
Nanak, "Why
didn't you join
in our prayers?"
"Because," said
Nanak, "Those
were not
prayers!"

"One of you was thinking about buying goats, and the other was buying horses in the marketplace. That is not praying." The two men were so astonished at Nanak's ability to read minds and know the truth, that they immediately became his disciples.

While traveling in Emnabad, Guru Nanak stopped to eat with a poor man named Lalo. A rich man named Bhago was very insulted and said, "You should eat my food instead, because it is much better!" Guru Nanak took a piece of Bhago's food in one hand, and then a piece of Lalo's in the other.

When he squeezed his fists, milk flowed from Lalo's food, but blood flowed from Bhago's. Guru Nanak said to Bhago, "Your rich food was gained by bleeding the poor. Lalo's was gained by honesty, good work, love, and true faith. Bhago! Your sins can be forgiven only by donating your wealth to the poor, and by living a life of honesty!"

Bhago was so amazed at Guru Nanak's miracle that he immediately shared his wealth and became one of Guru Nanak's greatest disciples.

At that time Barbar the Great was on the warpath and his army began to attack Emnabad. Thousands of people were about to be killed. Guru Nanak ran right up to Barbar's horse and grabbing the reigns shouted, "O Barbar! Stop this bloodshed!"

Barbar the Great's sword was raised, ready to strike, but he was so shocked by such valor and by seeing such a glowing spiritual face, that he did not harm Guru Nanak. Instead Guru Nanak was put in prison where he was forced to grind corn on millstones.

But in prison Guru Nanak performed yet another miracle!
When he started to sing, the other prisoners joined him, and
the millstones began to turn and grind the corn on their own.

Barbar the Great was again so astounded by the holy Guru's
miracle that he had to release him.

Guru Nanak traveled up to the Himalaya Mountains. In Haridwar, the great Ganga River begins to flow, and many Hindus would go into the river to wash away their sins, and throw water in the direction of the sun, believing this action would save their ancestors' souls in heaven. Guru Nanak asked the Hindus: "How far away are your ancestors from here?" The Hindus replied, "Many millions of miles!"

Guru Nanak then entered the river and began throwing water westwards. He said to the Hindus, "I am sprinkling my crops in the south. The water is sure to reach my crops, as they are much closer than are your ancestors!" Guru Nanak then said, "Do not practice empty rituals. With faith in God's Name, one saves the ancestors and the entire family. Those who love the beloved Name of God save themselves as well as their ancestors!"

One day Guru Nanak visited the great city of Lahore. The richest man there invited Guru Nanak to a sumptuous feast, boasting, "I am the wealthiest man here with the greatest luxuries of silver and gold, diamonds and rubies!" Guru Nanak said, "But you don't have this little needle. Keep it safe for me, and give it back to me when we meet again in heaven!"

The rich man asked, "But how can I take this needle with me to heaven when I die?"

"Exactly so!" said Guru Nanak, "You can't! Nor can you take all your riches and gold with you! They are all worthless!" The rich man realized the truth of Guru Nanak's words, and from that day on he gave away his riches to the poor, and was able to take his good deeds with him to heaven, when the time came, instead of a silly old needle.

Guru Nanak traveled through heatwaves and sandstorms, escaped robbers and drought, to reach the Muslim's holy city of Mecca. When he got there he was so tired that he immediately fell asleep, but his feet were facing the Muslim's holy house of God called the Kaaba. "How dare you sleep with your feet pointing to the Kaaba!" shouted the guards of the mosque. "Please forgive me and point my feet to whichever direction there is no God!" said Nanak.

But when the angry guards pulled Nanak's feet to the north, the Kaaba moved to the north. And the same happened when Nanak's feet were pulled to the south, to the east, and to the west. The guards then fell on their knees realizing he was a holy man. Nanak sang a hymn:

God is everywhere, in every direction.
And the true God is within.

After twenty-five years of traveling and spreading his message of peace and equality, Guru Nanak returned to his home in Kartapur.

On September 22, 1539, Guru Nanak told his followers that he would now depart from the mortal world. He covered himself with a white sheet, and his soul departed from his body. When the white sheet was removed, only beautiful fragrant flowers were seen in place of his body.

In death, Guru Nanak had shown that good deeds and the remembrance of God can make our life and our afterlife as beautiful as the fragrant flowers of his death shroud.

THE TRAVELS OF GURU NANAK

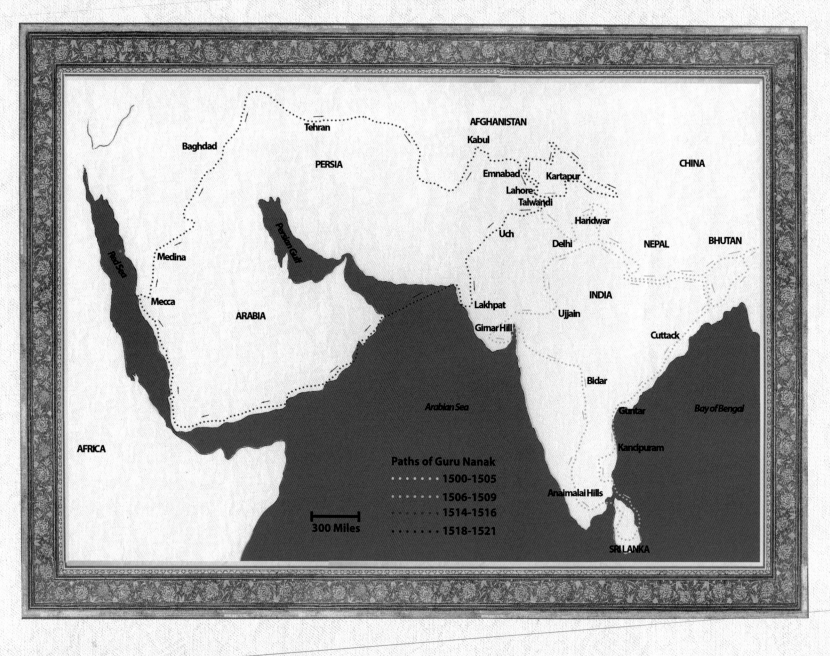

Baghdad

Tehran

AFGHANISTAN

Kabul

PERSIA

Emnabad

Kartapur

CHINA

Lahore

Talwandi

Haridwar

Red Sea

Medina

Uch

Delhi

NEPAL

BHUTAN

Mecca

ARABIA

Lakhpat

INDIA

Girnar Hill

Ujjain

Cuttack

Bidar

Arabian Sea

Guntar

Bay of Bengal

AFRICA

Kancipuram

Persian Gulf

Paths of Guru Nanak

· · · · · · 1500–1505

· · · · · · 1506–1509

· - · - · - 1514–1516

· · · · · · 1518–1521

Anaimalai Hills

300 Miles

SRI LANKA

ABOUT SIKHISM

❁ The Sikh religion originated in northwestern India in the late 15th century. It believes that there is one God, whose name is *Ik Onkar* (literally, "one God").

❁ Guru Nanak was the founder of Sikhism; he is the first of the Ten Sikh Gurus, or teachers, who lived from the years 1469-1708 and who revealed the sacred teachings of the religion.

❁ The holy book of Sikhism is called the *Guru Granth Sahib* ("Master Book by the Teacher") or *Adi Granth* ("First Book"); it contains the writings of the Ten Gurus. The scripture is considered an eternal living guru for Sikhs.

❁ A Sikh temple is called a gurdwara, meaning "the house of the guru." The Golden Temple in Amritsar, in north-western India, is the most famous Sikh temple and is covered in gold.

❁ Sikhs seek to practice the Three Pillars: 1. to meditate upon and chant God's Name (*naam japo*); 2. to earn their living honestly as a householder (*kirat karo*); and 3. to consume and share food and wealth with all, irrespective of caste, creed, or color (*vand chakko*).

❁ Sikhs strive to follow the Five Ks: 1. having uncut hair (*kesh*), which should be covered with a turban (for men) or a scarf (for women); 2. keeping a wooden comb (*kanga*) in their hair, symbolizing cleanliness; 3. wearing a steel bracelet (*kara*) for protection and showing that they are bound to the guru; 4. using cotton undergarments (*kachera*) as a reminder to stay away from lust and desire; and 5. carrying a small sword (*kirpan*) to defend their faith and protect the weak.

❁ Today Sikhs number approximately 25 million worldwide.

DATE DUE

For my mom, Marjorie Fisher, who gave me dreams
For Mark, who is the best thing that ever happened to me,
and for Sam and Stephanie, our double blessings
—M. O.

Margaret K. McElderry Books
An imprint of Simon & Schuster Children's Publishing Division
1230 Avenue of the Americas, New York, New York 10020
Text copyright © 2003 by Margaret O'Hair
Illustrations copyright © 2003 by Thierry Courtin
All rights reserved, including the right of reproduction in whole or in part in any form.
Book design by Ann Bobco and Kristin Smith
The text for this book is set in Rotis Serif.
The illustrations are rendered as digital art.
Manufactured in China
2 4 6 8 10 9 7 5 3 1
Library of Congress Cataloging-in-Publication Data
O'Hair, Margaret.
Twin to twin / by Margaret O'Hair ; illustrated by Thierry Courtin.— 1st ed.
p. cm.
Summary: A rhyming description of the
characteristics and activities of twin toddlers.
ISBN 0-689-84494-8
[1. Twins—Fiction. 2. Toddlers—Fiction. 3. Day—Fiction. 4. Stories in rhyme.]
I. Courtin, Thierry, ill. II. Title.
PZ8.3.O353 Tw 2003
[E]—dc21
2001031723

FIRST
EDITION